Astronomy Now!™

A Look at
VENUS

Mary R. Dunn

PowerKiDS press.

New York

Dedicated to my dear friend, Helen

Published in 2008 by The Rosen Publishing Group, Inc.
29 East 21st Street, New York, NY 10010

First Edition

Editor: Amelie von Zumbusch
Book Design: Greg Tucker
Photo Researcher: Nicole Pristash

Photo Credits: Cover, pp. 17 (main), 19 Courtesy NASA/JPL-Caltech; pp. 5, 7 (main) by Digital Vision; pp. 7 (top inset), 11 by Photodisc; pp. 7 (bottom inset), 12 © Shutterstock.com; p. 9, 13 (top inset), 15, 17 (inset), 21 (inset) © Getty Images; pp. 13 (bottom inset), 21 (main) by NASA; p. 17 (main) Courtesy NASA/JPL-Caltech.

Library of Congress Cataloging-in-Publication Data

Dunn, Mary R.
  A look at Venus / Mary R. Dunn. — 1st ed.
      p. cm. — (Astronomy now!)
  Includes index.
  ISBN-13: 978-1-4042-3826-8 (library binding)
  ISBN-10: 1-4042-3826-3 (library binding)
  1. Venus (Planet)—Juvenile literature. I. Title.
  QB621.D855 2008
  523.42—dc22
                                    2007002331

Manufactured in the United States of America

Contents

Earth's Sister Planet

The **planet** Venus is sometimes called Earth's twin or sister because it is about the same size as Earth. Venus also has many of the same landforms Earth has, such as mountains, plains, and valleys.

In our **solar system**, Venus is the second planet from the Sun. Venus is the brightest planet in our solar system. During part of the year, Venus moves toward Earth. Throughout this time, you can see Venus glowing like a star in the night sky. The other part of the year, Venus moves away from Earth. Then, Venus can often be seen in the morning sky.

Although it is a planet, Venus is sometimes called the morning star or the evening star. This is because it shines so brightly in the early morning and the evening.

Venus's Orbit

Venus travels around the Sun in a nearly circle-shaped path, called an orbit. It takes Venus one Venusian year, or 225 days, to orbit the Sun. A Venusian year is 140 days shorter than a year on Earth.

Sometimes, Venus passes between the Sun and Earth. This passing is called a transit. Long ago, **scientists** discovered that if they measured Venus's transit from many different places on Earth, they could figure out how far Earth is from the Sun. Scientists still use Venus's transits to study the planets. The next transit of Venus will happen on June 6, 2012.

Venus is the second planet from the Sun. It is also the closest planet to Earth. *Inset:* The black dot you can see here is Venus crossing the Sun during a transit of Venus.

Venus's Axis

As Venus orbits the Sun, it spins in the **opposite** direction on its axis. An axis is a pretend line through a planet's center. The time it takes Venus to spin all the way around is one day on Venus. Venus spins so slowly that one day there lasts as long as 243 days on Earth.

Venus's spinning makes the Sun rise in the west and set in the east there. The opposite is true on Earth, where the Sun rises in the east and sets in the west. Some scientists think Venus once spun as Earth does. They believe something big crashed into Venus and changed the way it spins on its axis.

It is daytime on the side of Venus that faces the Sun. It is night on the side that the Sun's light does not reach. As Venus spins, it becomes day or night on different parts of the planet.

9

Looking at Venus

From Earth, Venus looks very bright because the Sun's light makes it shine. However, scientists have trouble getting a close look at Venus, even with a **telescope**. This is because thick, spinning, yellow clouds cover the planet.

Venus's clouds are different from Earth's clouds. While Earth's clouds are mostly water, Venus's clouds are made of **acid**. Strong winds of up to 220 miles per hour (354 km/h) push the clouds around Venus. Scientists study what Venus looks like below the clouds with spacecraft. The spacecraft send radio waves through the clouds and take pictures of Venus to send back to Earth.

A spacecraft took this picture of the planet Venus and sent the picture back to Earth.

11

Cool Facts

Venus is named for the Roman goddess of love and beauty.

Venus
Venus has no moons or rings.

Venus is the only planet that has pancake domes. These strange, pancakelike landforms are miles (km) across and miles (km) high.

A day on Venus lasts as long as 243 days on Earth. This is longer than it takes Venus to go around the Sun!

Earth's orbit takes it nearer to Venus than to any other planet.

A Venus Timeline

2006 - The *Venus Express* reaches Venus on April 11.

1989 - Scientists send *Magellan* to learn about Venus.

1962 - *Mariner 2* is sent off to gather facts about Venus.

1639 - Jeremiah Horrocks and William Crabtree watch the first recorded transit of Venus on December 4.

1610 - Galileo Galilei starts watching Venus. His records of Venus's shape help prove that Venus and the other planets move around the Sun.

Fun Figures

A group of mountains on Venus, called Maxwell Montes, are 7 miles (11 km) high and 540 miles (870 km) long.

Venus is 7,520 miles (12,102 km) across.

Venus is about 67 million miles (108 million km) from the Sun.

13

The Air on Venus

From pictures taken by spacecraft, scientists also know that Venus is very hot. Venus's thick clouds trap the Sun's heat. This is much like the **greenhouse effect** on Earth. It makes Venus very hot. The planet can be as hot as 870° F (466° C).

Besides being very hot, Venus also has high **atmospheric pressure**. The atmospheric pressure on Venus pushes down about 90 times more strongly than it does on Earth. The pressure is so powerful that it would flatten a spacecraft in under a day if it landed on the **surface** of Venus.

Venus's clouds are made up mostly of sulfuric acid. This is a kind of matter that is very unsafe for people.

15

Landforms on Venus

Like Earth, Venus has mountains and **volcanoes**. Venus also has bowl-like forms called craters. Craters form when rocks crash into a planet. Venus has fewer craters than Mercury and Mars do. Scientists think this is because Venus's surface has changed more than that of other planets. They also think Venus's thick clouds might keep some of the rocks that fly by from reaching Venus.

Landforms on Venus are named for important women. A deep valley is named for the Roman hunting goddess Diana. Another landform is named for Sacajawea, a Native American woman who guided the **explorers** Lewis and Clark.

Crater Isabella, seen here, is the second-largest crater on Venus. *Inset:* Crater Isabella is named after Queen Isabella of Castile. Isabella was the Spanish queen who backed the first European trip to America.

More Landforms on Venus

Venus has some landforms that are not found on Earth. For example, Venus has big, round, crownlike shapes called coronae. Coronae can be more than 100 miles (160 km) wide. Scientists think coronae formed when hot matter from inside the planet came to the surface. Venus also has raised places that look like hills and valleys that formed in different directions. These are called tesserae.

Scientists think that the crust, or outside, of Venus may not be fully hard. They believe that the crust may be able to change shape and move around over time.

The biggest of Venus's coronae is Artemis Corona, shown here. It is more than 1,250 miles (2,000 km) wide.

19

Visiting Venus

Spacecraft have taught scientists a lot about Venus. In the 1960s, an American spacecraft named *Mariner 2* traveled near Venus. It sent back pictures to Earth. It helped scientists discover that the planet is very hot and always has clouds around it. In the 1970s, the Russian spacecraft *Venera* took pictures of Venus. It looked for signs of water and measured how fast the wind blew.

Magellan, another American spacecraft, orbited Venus in the 1990s. It helped scientists map Venus's surface. They even let the spacecraft crash-land on Venus to find out more about the planet's thick clouds!

Scientists on the *Atlantis*, seen here, sent *Magellan* off to Venus on May 4, 1989. *Inset:* After reaching Venus, *Magellan* sent pictures of the planet's surface back to Earth.

21

Learning More About Venus

In 2005, scientists sent off a spacecraft called *Venus Express* to learn more about Earth's nearest neighbor. *Venus Express* began orbiting Venus in April 2006. It studied the planet's air, clouds, mountains, and craters. Scientists still want to know many more things about Venus. They want to find out if Venus ever had water. They want to see if the heat on Venus is the reason it is not more like Earth.

Scientists believe that learning about Venus will help them understand Earth better, too. Knowledge of Venus could even help us deal with the greenhouse effect on our planet.

Glossary

acid (A-sud) A kind of matter that breaks down matter faster than water does.

atmospheric pressure (at-muh-SFEER-ik PREH-shur) The weight of the air pressing down on something.

explorers (ek-SPLOR-urz) People who travel and look for new land.

greenhouse effect (GREEN-hows eh-FEKT) When gases in the air around Earth trap heat near Earth's surface.

opposite (O-puh-zet) Totally and exactly different.

planet (PLA-net) A large object, such as Earth, that moves around the Sun.

scientists (SY-un-tists) People who study the world.

solar system (SOH-ler SIS-tem) A group of planets that circles a star.

surface (SER-fes) The outside of anything.

telescope (TEH-leh-skohp) A tool used to make faraway objects appear closer and larger.

volcanoes (vol-KAY-nohz) Openings in the surface of a planet that sometimes shoot up hot melted rock called lava.

Index

A

atmospheric pressure, 14

C

clouds, 10, 14, 16, 20, 22

D

day(s), 6, 8
direction(s), 8, 18

G

greenhouse effect, 14, 22

L

landform(s), 4, 16, 18

M

mountains, 4, 16, 22

P

plains, 4

S

scientists, 6, 8, 10, 14, 18, 20, 22
solar system, 4
star, 4
Sun, 4, 6, 8

surface, 14, 16, 20

T

telescope, 10
transit, 6

V

valley(s), 4, 16, 18
volcanoes, 16

W

water, 10, 20, 22

Y

year, 4, 6

Web Sites

Due to the changing nature of Internet links, PowerKids Press has developed an online list of Web sites related to the subject of this book. This site is updated regularly. Please use this link to access the list: www.powerkidslinks.com/astro/venus/